ONENESS IS THE PITS

Written and Illustrated

by

BETTY E. WIENER

Edited by

MARY ELIZABETH KRAUEL

THE WRITER'S SERVICE PUBLICATIONS

Shreveport, Louisiana

First Printing, 1991
Second Printing, 1991
Third Printing, 1991

Published by The Writer's Service Publications

For information, please contact:

Mary Elizabeth Krauel
The Writer's Service
816 Pierremont Road
Shreveport, LA 71106
(318) 869-3587

Printed in the United States of America
by
Sanders Printing Co.
Garretson, South Dakota

ISBN 0-9629007-0-2

CONTENTS

FOREWARD

During my senior year in high school in Little Rock, Arkansas, I had a course in Creative Writing. The teacher, Miss Cecelia Murphy, admonished us always to write something about which we know.

At the time, I spent the semester cartooning the class and Miss Murphy.

In the many years that followed, I continued to cartoon situations and acquaintances. My card club will recall on two occasions, with a passage of intervening years between the first and the second, I drew them all as the animal they most resembled.

Recently, however, my life changed, and I was prompted to write about situations I REALLY have experienced. Thus, a collection of these experiences has become *ONENESS IS THE PITS.*

Many of my friends will identify with some instances, especially those who were participants.

So, any resemblance to persons living is NOT coincidental.

Betty Wiener

"If You Haven't Been There, You Will"

1

IF YOU HAVEN'T BEEN THERE, YOU WILL

What is it with this brain of mine?
Is it of some bizarre design?
My days are filled with NO recall
(For names of friends, I slowly stall).

And up and down the stairs I go,
What for? I do not seem to know.
But . . . once in bed for needed rest,
Suddenly, instant mental zest!

Lamenting minute things undone,
The clock glares back from ten 'til one . . .
A need to check utilities,
The gas, the locks--futilities.

And then, a list of things to do
(The hands are slowly passing two),
That melody you finally name
Was the favorite of your teen-aged flame.

Everything is as clear as day
Remembering the night away,
But, lo, 'ere the morning comes
What was that tune he always hummed?

"The Truth"

THE TRUTH

SADDEST SIGHT UNDER THE SUN
IS A PULLEY BONE FOR ONE.

"My Dog"

MY DOG

What do you do with the bossy pet
Your friends persuaded you to get?
They said, "Everyone needs a Rover,"
But he has completely taken over!

No privacy, aye, there's the rub;
He even tried to share my tub,
But the nights are especially tough--
One kingsize bed's not BIG enough!

"Facelift"

FACELIFT

My mirror, mirror on the wall
Suddenly now has the gall
To tell me what my image found;
Really, I'm a basset hound!

Jowls and wrinkles, sad to say,
Creams and masques cannot allay.
My oldest friend appears sixteen,
Her facelift made a beauty queen.

I plunge right in and call a surgeon;
Heretofore, I'd need urgin'.
He managed just to "squeeze me in,"
A modest fee, and we begin.

Instantly, I have a ball
As I absorb the pentothal.
I wish someone had given warning
What I would look like come mid-morning.
Bandaged up as Carmen Miranda,
My eyes behold a giant panda.

Then . . .
Two weeks later a guy gets mushy
(Another even pats my tushy!)
A lovely, younger "me" I see,
Neck down, there's still the REST of me.

"Invitations"

INVITATIONS

Invited to a dinner dance,
My pulse quickens at the chance
To jitterbug and do the twist,
But on arrival . . . get the gist . . .

Five women for each single man.
However, I devise a plan:
We'll put them on the auction block
And bid until we're all in hock.

My purchase soon did burst my bubble--
His two-step wasn't worth the trouble.

"The Health Club"

THE HEALTH CLUB

By the shores of health club waters,
By the gruesome stretch machine,
Seniors puffing with their daughters
Aiming to be tall and lean.

Now the time for waistline measure,
A "ten" is bound to be a cinch.
All this torture for the pleasure
To subtract a quarter inch!

"Big Expenditure"

BIG EXPENDITURE

My new car makes me quite ecstatic
But driving it a bit erratic.
Dashboard blinking! Lights and bells--
On these my concentration dwells.

I didn't see the barricade;
I hit it hard, and there I stayed.
The tow truck came; I waved bye-bye . . .
Can't let him see a big girl cry!

"Dates"

DATES

I can't be picky,
A date's a date
My palms are sticky;
He isn't late.

There's one thing I hate
As I glance at the floor;
My shoes are an eight,
HIS shoes are a four!

"Golf"

GOLF

My dream to be on the sports page
Is achieved at last in my old age
In newsprint. My golfing dream?
Not my score, as it should seem.

I killed a snake on number two
So my foursome could play through!
Two nine-iron shots were his demise--
They gave me par as the hero's prize.

"Eggs"

EGGS

The whites from separated eggs
We always had in our possession
For desserts and spectacular meringue--
Before the cholesterol obsession.

But now the chefs, poor saddened fellows,
Are left with all the useless yellows.

"Opera Guild Style Show"

OPERA GUILD STYLE SHOW

Who do they think will wear 'em?
'Cause the matrons attending,
Not wildest dreams bending,
On a desert island would dare 'em!

"Groceries For One"

GROCERIES FOR ONE

At first you're embarrassed to buy one potato
Or onion or grapefruit or even tomato.

The butcher's glare makes you go limp
While he weighs your half-dozen shrimp.

But his patience really comes undone
When he has to carve a roast for ONE!

"Aspen"

25

ASPEN

Incentive to ski:
OVER SEVENTY . . . FREE!

"Fitness"

FITNESS

I plan my walks at break of day;
The park is just a block away.
Maybe meet a handsome stranger
Or some defenseless park ranger.

To catch an unsuspecting brute
I don my sexy jogging suit,
The suit that shows my youngish fanny.
He smiles and says, "Good morning, Granny."

"Wedding Reception"

WEDDING RECEPTION

You're seated at place-carded table,
Arranged as best the host was able,
"Oh, don't mind me, feel free to dance,"
You smile and around the room you glance.

Then, "Vant to dence?" loose plates do muffle,
It's the old retirement village shuffle.
You're on the floor, no need to fuss,
You dance and try to miss his truss.

You're tagged, a silent thanks to heaven,
Oh, no! It's Irwin, age eleven,
Earning points for his Boy Scout troop
As we do the loop de loop.

"A Costly Mistake"

A COSTLY MISTAKE

I attempt to remake
With cream and mascara,
Yet, hard as I try
I'm no Scarlett O'Hara.

But the error so big
Is a blonde curly wig,
And my mirror reflects no joy--

Alas and alack,
The one who looks back
Is Little Lord Faunt-le-roy!

"Season's Greetings"

SEASON'S GREETINGS

Long Xeroxed Christmas letters
Of detailed travels through the year,
The litters of all the family pets
To evoke some mutual cheer.

And surgery, and Disneyland,
Children's grades, a swollen gland . . .
How to answer such a greeting
Without disclosing interest fleeting?

"Hypochondria Syndrome"

HYPOCHONDRIA SYNDROME

More often now I take my pulses,
I, who handled kids' convulses.
I magnify that little pain
To, "Maybe I have a tumored brain!"

But, as my time begins to fill,
I find I am no longer ill.
Some bargain sales, a few old males,
And suddenly my "illness" pales.

"High Heels"

HIGH HEELS

A sad aspect of aging news
When going out to shop for shoes
Is the sorrow that one feels
In having to forego high heels.

But if you find the flesh is weak,
You'll even hobble up Pikes Peak.
You're stupid, heaven only knows,
High heels weren't made for hammer toes!

"Shopping Trip"

SHOPPING TRIP

Kay and Jane, Louise and Alice
Each December drive to Dallas.
Three hours it takes to cross the isthmus
From our town, to shop for Christmas.

This year everything went well
'Til coming home--the car did tell
Impending doom, as engine sputtered,
After which ne'er sound it uttered.

We talked it over--not to panic,
Two hitched a ride to find mechanic.
After a time, a change of luck;
From nearby came a towing truck.

He hitched us backwards at an angle
We didn't even mind the dangle.
Picture us a happy bunch
While we ate our picnic lunch.

Passing truckers laughed and waved
As our unique trip we braved.

"Where Did They Go?"

WHERE DID THEY GO?

Beauticians with their vats of bluing
All gray-headed customers pursuing.
In decades past . . .
They did them all,
The fat, the thin, the short, the tall.

But blue-haired ladies are no more,
A different sameness is the score.
Now, they all sport pale blonde tresses.
Can it be there are less stresses?

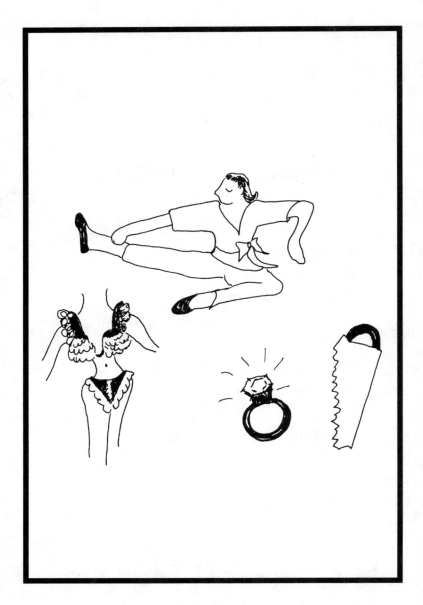

"Shopping By Mail"

SHOPPING BY MAIL

Catalogs daily by the ton
Weird, the gamut that they run
With no regard for age or gender,
The glowing ads--a spirit mender.

As we browse, our fancies soar--
Sexy nighties, gems galore,
Security systems, auto parts,
Or a course in martial arts.
Gourmet gadgets, menus styled,
So I can rival Julia Child!

Place an order . . . sad to say
Six weeks later, to the day,
Wrong size and nothing like the picture!
My pressure almost causes stricture.

What to do? Alas, alack,
Just DO NOT try to send it back!

"Modern-Day Physical"

45

MODERN-DAY PHYSICAL

Whatever happened to the one-day physical?
After week-long tests, you're quizzical.
For all your parts the specialty boys
Trot out their procedural toys.

Echo for your heart, Paps for your tubes,
Mammogram programmed just for boobs.
Bone-scan called an M.R.I.
(If you're claustrophobic, you'll just die).

A huge machine with awesome tunnel,
(You enter the small end of the funnel).
Four other scans of varying type
With dye injected for nuclear hype.

The chart proclaims my actual age,
A Medicare number sets the stage,
But each technician asks me SERIOUSLY,
"Are you pregnant?" I laugh deliriously!

How many patients come in stable
But become critical on the table?
The doctor orders one more test
(To put his insurer's mind at rest).

By now, with gritted teeth
(There is no spit to foam),
Drive straightway to the bank
And put a MORTGAGE on your home.

"Locked Out"

LOCKED OUT

Locked out--no need to ring the bell
No one's there to hear me yell.
Casement windows not ajar . . .
Resigned, I bed down in the car.

A cruising cop drives past, I see;
Will he buy, "Forgot my key"?

"Act Your Age"

ACT YOUR AGE

"Don't set your sights on a guy with curls,"
Is my advice to the Medicare girls.
Avoid the touted singles bars,
And go for the guys with the by-pass scars!

"Phone Calls"

PHONE CALLS

Solicitors of every ilk
From graveyard plots to beauty milk,
Garbage bags, Policemen's Ball,
(One even had the utter gall
To offer cut-rate cremation--
With chances on a CRUISE VACATION!)

Finally, came an obscene one,
By now, my patience quite undone,
I spewed out all the smut I'd known;
The caller quickly dropped the phone.

"Fact of Life"

FACT OF LIFE

I had a date with a younger man
For which I was delighted.
With beauty aids I set the stage--
I really didn't look my age.

But just before he rang the bell . . .

The grandkids came in daddy's truck;
And, as usual, they ran amuck.
With one fell swoop, they broke the spell--
My years piled right back on as well.

"Check-Up"

CHECK-UP

So . . . I'll try the fitness test
Today, I feel I'm at my best.
Sad to say, a BAD mistake
The nurses my calculations make.

Cholesterol, a mere three hundred,
Blood pressure out of reason thundered,
My weight surely must be less . . .
Diagnosis: I'm a MESS!

"Nightmare Relived"

NIGHTMARE RELIVED

I should have stayed at home that day
When I put the brisket on to bake.
Company was on the way;
I'd made the usual icebox cake.

From bridge I phone the maid at two--
"Is the roast tender through and through?"
"Yes, it is," came her reply.
"It's quite tender, but it's BLUE!"

I fled the game despite their pleas,
At home called forth all my restraint,
On viewing the entree's rare disease,
I didn't have the time to faint.

I whittled off the outer crust,
My *Kitchen Bouquet* I had to trust.
Though the bluest part I had to ditch,
The meal went off without a hitch.

The mystery solved . . . I'd tinted undies,
Badly needed for a month of Sundays,
Granite roaster, the perfect pot,
Guess the RINSING I forgot!

"Ms. Fixit"

MS. FIXIT

I light the pilots spring and fall,
Unclog the sink, light upper hall.
I even bought a hand-held sander,
Also trapped a salamander.

Can't understand the female flap,
Removing mousie from the trap,
But when my ring went down the drain,
The gooseneck wasn't my domain.

I know I've accomplished things much dumber,
But I DO know when to call the plumber!

"Preparing For Summer"

PREPARING FOR SUMMER

The dressing room mirror is cruelly cutting,
Revealing the place my body is jutting . . .
The cut up the pelvis designed where it hurts,
Whatever happened to bathing suit skirts?

"Unexpected Guests"

UNEXPECTED GUESTS

Why won't friends phone before they call?
The doorbell rings; I cannot stall.
And so I hide behind a chair
With Clairol dye upon my hair.

"Dumped"

DUMPED

She isn't younger,
I am prettier--
I fish and golf,
And I'm so much wittier.

I helped him recall things he forgot
Even found a parking lot.

I guess I made a big mistake;
Dependency, I couldn't fake.
I offered to help him all I can,
But she calls him her "Macho Man."

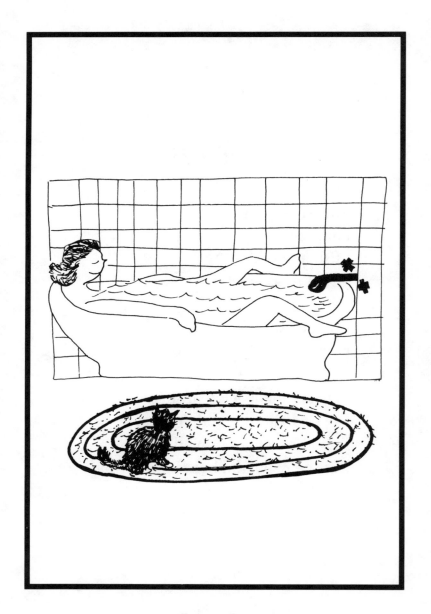

"Poison Ivy"

POISON IVY

I guess I didn't use my head
While planting bulbs divine,
Squatting in the tulip bed,
Ignoring poison ivy vine.

But later on, a scarlet patch,
A frantic call for help for me.
Where it isn't ladylike to scratch
My doctor said, "Come let me see."

A phone prescription was my plea--

His answer was an oatmeal bath,
Which was a blessing in disguise.
Since to my tub I beat a path,
Cholesterol has ceased to rise.

"Predicament"

PREDICAMENT

My stylishly long earring dangles,
My tight dress overhead entangles.
Can't get it up,
Can't get it down.
Got the feeling: 'bout to drown!
Doesn't help to call on heaven;
Clutch the phone for nine-eleven.

"The Wellness Clinic Group"

THE WELLNESS CLINIC GROUP

At wellness clinic, all work out,
The crowd's diverse, there is no doubt.
All ages, physiques, and professions,
Improving bodies, the obsession.

Outfits vary--sweats and shorts,
The stylish look this group sports,
But when they meet in other places
Attempt to match the clothes and faces.

Meeting at a cocktail feast--
Bursted bubble . . . he's a PRIEST!

"Daytime Drama"

DAYTIME DRAMA

I really want it to be me--
I know it's silly when
I watch the clinches on Channel Three
Of all the leading men.

Close-ups of their smooth caresses,
When my heart of hearts confesses
Dreams of being slightly shady--
The soap opera's leading lady.

"Going Places"

GOING PLACES

Called for by a pair of older friends,
Wondering what he or she intends.
Wifey usually does the driving--
For proper manners I am striving.

Will he get out and ring the bell?
Only dragging time will tell.
I guess it's best to save his pride . . .
I'll don my coat and wait outside.

In the drive I softly hum . . . .
Oh dear, my ride FORGOT to come.

"Gypsy Gyp"

GYPSY GYP

I sought a gypsy fortune teller
To learn if I would get a feller.
Thought she might even have some views
On the perfect time to take a cruise.

So . . . what she saw within my palm
She blurted out without a qualm:
"Madame, you vill be exotic dancer
And so soon vill know da answer
To your heart's vildest dreem--
You vill make da Broadvay scene!
Compared to you at the top,
Gypsy Rose was qvite a flop."

My fortune rivals Barbara Hutton;
I have a SUPER belly button!

"Bridge"

BRIDGE

"Did you hear the news about Sue?"
"I hear she certainly got her due."
The bridge table conversation
Often leads to misinformation!

"Traveling"

TRAVELING

Airports' fiendish intentions
Spawn the drawbacks of traveling
And a shortage of comfort inventions,
The body and soul are unraveling.

Unloading at Gate Number One,
Departing at Gate Forty-two
With only ten minutes, I RUN,
My varicose veins are quite blue.

"Second Time Around"

SECOND TIME AROUND

Our hair is gray and somewhat thin
I've tried so hard your heart to win.
(I've known you since you first wore braces)
Passing years have left few traces.
And though we went our separate ways,
Fate has some funny tricks she plays.

Let's let the grandkids go their ways
And relish our remaining days.
Old cupid has surely shot his arrow
Into my arteries so narrow!

"Finale"

85

FINALE

I know I've painted "onesome" gruesome,
But now, again, I am a twosome.
We've lighted romance's tiny ember
And helped each other to remember.

"A big bed," Dr. Ruth espouses,
But our "l'affair grand" enjoys TWO houses.